Why Is There a Universal Hate for GOD?

Pastor Freddie E. Dixson Sr.

ISBN 979-8-88943-836-6 (paperback)
ISBN 979-8-88943-837-3 (digital)

Copyright © 2024 by Pastor Freddie E. Dixson Sr.

All rights reserved. No part of this publication may be reproduced, distributed, or transmitted in any form or by any means, including photocopying, recording, or other electronic or mechanical methods without the prior written permission of the publisher. For permission requests, solicit the publisher via the address below.

Christian Faith Publishing
832 Park Avenue
Meadville, PA 16335
www.christianfaithpublishing.com

Printed in the United States of America

Contents

Introduction

Too much and never enough—it's for the needy and not the greedy. The devil himself is trying his best to threaten the world's health economic security and social fabric. I personally spent much time praying and observing the traits and the work of the devil and his effect upon this entire universe.

I thank God, first and foremost, for saving my life through His Son Jesus Christ. I owe Him my all. I have surrendered my life to Him, which means that my life is in His hands and all of those who trust in Him as their only hope in this world. And secondly, I thank God for the beautiful and lovely saved wife that God has blessed me with until death do us part, along with my two handsome and truly saved sons God has blessed us with. I also acknowledge my beautiful and respectful four grandchildren that God has also blessed us with.

I thank God for my wonderful daughter-in-law. What a blessing to have such a blessed daughter-in-law. My son Dedric and all of us are grateful for each other. I thank God all the time for the people He has placed in my life: Bro. Willie Mcquire and his wife, Sis. Gloria Mcquire, and their grandchildren. To my family and relatives and my church family, for their love and continuous support of the hard work that God has allowed me to accomplish.

Again, I thank God for my beautiful wife, who works along my side to help and encourage me to write this book. But most importantly, I thank God for giving me the wisdom and the know-how on when to start writing this book. I thank my late mother, Sis. Angelette Winford Dixson, and my daddy, Rev. Walter Dixson Sr., for the Christian upbringing. They taught me all about Jesus and His love for all. I would now like to share with the world this book.

He that Committeth sin is of the devil; for the devil sinneth from the beginning. For this purpose the Son of God was manifested, that he might destroy the works of the devil. (1 John 3:8)

If the soul is left in darkness, sins will be committed.

The guilty one is not the one who commits the sin, but the one who causes the darkness.

Much of this book comes from the wisdom and knowledge that comes from God Himself (*James 1:5, 17*). For every event during which I observed, I was present. I relied on the *Holy Spirit*, which helps me to record much of the events that God only allows me to record. I've reconstructed some dialogue according to what I personally remember; what I have seen, witnessed, and heard; and what I allow the *Holy Spirit* to bring into my remembrance. I have always been one who is a positive thinker. I try my best to have the mind of Christ as the apostle Paul says in *Philippians 2:5*.

I truly thank God for His revelatory knowledge of the devil and those who have the mind of the devil. I'm not simply calling anyone the devil. I'll allow the Word of God to speak for itself (*John 8:32, 44–47*). We are living in a world where many people do not acknowledge the one and only one who created them—the God of the universe (Genesis 1:1, 26–27).

Too many people who are in high positions are operating from their own intellect and using their own power for their personal gain. There are those in the political realm or field who try to replace God and never acknowledge Him or accepted Him as their savior. Don't get me wrong, I'm not the true judge. I'm just a fruit inspector (Matthew 7:20–23).

There are many folks who are trying to run this country in sin. They don't realize that you cannot lead where you don't go, and you cannot teach what you don't know. When God created this world, His intention was for everyone and everything that He created. He created the world because *He loved us all,* no matter *our color, race, creed, ethics, culture, background, religion, etc.* God created us all in His image and His likeness *(Genesis 1:26–28).*

Then the question we all need to ask ourselves: What causes all the *hate, the separation, the murders, envy, disputes, the lying tongues, the mistreating of one another, the cheating, and the division in our country when this is supposed to be the United States of America? The devil always talks about saving America.* Satan, I pass notice on you this day! You cannot save America or any other country if you are not saved yourself. *Talk is cheap.* Now the answer to the question is found in *Genesis 3:1–24.* The devil himself has a great deal of information about all of us who ever lived and is still living in this sinful world. Who is trying to make things right? The question to that is only for those who want to do what's right in the eyes of God and His people *(the saved).* We already know that the devil sinned and lied way before the beginning of creation, and everyone who follows him are part of him, which means they are sinners and liars just as the devil is. The truth is not in you if all you do is lie, lie, lie.

Maybe, you could by your on inclinations are born a liar *(Psalm 58:3; 51:5). Just to remind this old world, whatever you do or say, good or bad, you can never replace the God of this universe.* Now, I really want to help many people if I can. I know I won't be helping everybody because everybody doesn't have the mind of Christ, and everybody just simply doesn't care or believe in God *(Matthew 7:21–23).* But I'm held accountable to tell *God's loving truth.* You will never be free of yourselves until you know the truth, the whole truth, and nothing but the truth *(John 8:32).* I honor only what the Word of God says to me *(Romans 13:1–3).* We are to obey or be subject to the higher powers. Everyone who takes an *oath* is saying these words or similar to these:

> I do solemnly swear that I will support and
> defend the Constitution of the United States
> against all enemies, foreign and domestic, that I
> will bear truth faith and allegiance to the same;
> that I take this obligation freely, without any

mental reservation or purpose of evasion, and I
will well and faithfully discharge.

Really? Now, you tell me who that sounds like. It sounds like the
one who defrauded his way into the White House, only to do corruption and manipulate the system just to have a bunch of his blinded
followers to do his dirty work. Well, if you're stuck on ignorance
and you don't have the wisdom of God, you'll just believe in anything your leader says or tells you to do, even if it's a lie. Everybody
can't accept the fact that they are weak. *What this world really needs
is prayer.* I pray for everyone—the good, the bad, the rich, and the
poor; it doesn't matter. I don't have the power to change anyone, but
I do know someone who can *(Jesus)*.

Sometimes, I pray for the place where all the presidents are
(notice that I say "the presidents" not "the dictators"). I pray that the
name White House will be changed to the *Right House* because what
I have observed all of my life is that many people who are elected as
president, not dictators, uses the White House to hide and do their
dirty deeds. To be honest, everything started way back in November
17, 1800. Everything seemed to be going just fine until the devil got
in, not by a landslide. I believe it was by fraud! This is why the *big lie*
is out. Satan is a liar and a great deceiver *(Revelation 12:9)*.

And to tell you the truth, many of his followers have the mark
of the beast *(Revelation 13:16–17)*. *They worship this beast.* As quiet
as it is kept, your own family members can make a monster out of
you. Sometimes, a person can become the primary source of solace
when they are much more likely to be a source of fear or rejection.
It puts you into an intolerable position, being totally dependent on
your parents, who are also likely to be a source of your terror.

Child abuse is, in some sense, the experience of "too much"
or "not enough," and some people directly experienced the "not
enough" in the loss of connection to their parents, especially at a crucial developmental stage, which can be deeply traumatic. Without
warning, your needs aren't being met, and your fears and longings
go unsoothed. It goes to show that you can't always depend on your

parents. You have to really depend on God, but if you don't know God, how are you going to depend on Him? *I guess your answer is me!*

This is one of the reasons the people in this world are all messed up: it's all about them. The people are divided because mostly everyone wants power, money, and prestige, but not everyone believes in the One with all powers. If God doesn't take you to the top His way, then the top is not a safe place for you. And if the Lord doesn't give it to you, then it is a dangerous thing to have.

Remember that the love of money is the root of all evil. If this describes, you then you better be very careful. It costs you to live but twice as much to leave, if you know what I mean. I have found out down through the years that if your house is not right, it is a possibility that you will not be right. People just like to have their way all the time. People are not who they claim to be. They talk a good conversation but have no demonstration. People treat others with disrespect, and nickel-and-diming them make them look tough. We have people who are not even aware of solving their own problems, but they are great in creating problems for others.

Now, enough of that. Now, here is the real deal: whether you accept it or not, what you believe and receive determines how you behave. We have in the White House a president and a vice president, who are trying their best to do what's right for the people of *the United States of America*. I must say they are not perfect; none of us is. But by observing, I see a whole lot of some great things that really bless a lot of the people of America. This president has won the election fairly, no matter what big lie is out. President Joe Biden and Vice President Mrs. Kamala Harris have been in office for thirteen months, and they and their staff accomplished more in thirteen months than the former guy did in four years. You can call it what you want, but I need to explain to you more about the devil.

Whether you want to accept it or not, that's your prerogative. I'm just a voice, God's mouthpiece. Anyway, the devil's job is to steal, kill, and destroy *(John 10:10)*, and he knows that he cannot be everywhere like the Lord can. God is omnipresent. He's everywhere at the same time *(Proverbs 15:3)*. He's watching everything the people in this world is doing, whether you are rich, poor, saved, or unsaved.

God never sleeps. The devil creeped his way not just in the Garden of Eden, but also into the White House. The purpose of him coming into the White House is to steal, kill, and destroy.

You might ask, What is he destroying? I really don't have to answer that, but anybody who is in their right mind *(the mind of Christ)*, you already know what he came to do. Just take a look, not a long hard look, at what's all going on in *the universe.* I've never, in all my lifetime, seen so much terrible and horrible, devious, devilish evil and wickedness going on in the universe. It appears to me that as soon as Satan entered the Garden of Eden, he began to lead his own into a world of deep sin. As soon as Satan left the White House, all hell broke out. The so-called GOP was fighting against the Democrats, and the leader of the pack, with such a corrupt mind, had the audacity to call names toward his what you call enemies.

Don't forget that earlier I told you that the devil is a liar and a great deceiver. He has poisoned the minds of his followers, and all he cares about is himself. He doesn't even care about his followers at all as long as they are doing his evil deeds. That's all that matters to him. Satan is very crafty and cunning. Satan was in the White House, but not in the right house *(God's house of prayer)*.

Come on, people, get smart. Satan also came to destroy our real intelligence.

Adam and Eve knew that they were naked *(Genesis 3:7)*. "Knew" means they became "physically or sensually aware." Their senses suddenly took on leadership, and as a result, the soul became alive without the Spirit directing it.

Man began to live from the outside instead of the inside. Adam and Eve became aware of their nakedness. They became aware of the leaves that could be used to cover themselves. They became conscious of shame and fear—the things that came from the outside, from the intellect.

Again, Satan destroyed man's true intelligence, which is a spiritual relationship with God. When we are connected with God, our spirits know anything and everything. That's why the knowledge on how God communicates is not learned. It is discerned. The knowledge of God isn't found in any books; it's a deeper knowledge. Your real intelligence is not studied; it's discerned. Wow!

When man lost his relationship with God, he became a victim of education. He began to look into books and movies and the words of others—what he can see, hear, taste, feel, and touch—to gain knowledge. Those things became our sources of information.

When Satan destroyed our real intelligence, we looked outside ourselves to find knowledge; by destroying our relationship with God, Satan capped off our life potential. He continually destroys any possibility that we might become more than we already are; Satan sets us up. Satan chops up our self-confidence and slams the door on our potential by convincing us that we are nothing.

The devil has been teaching and preaching that to keep us down. He is very skilled at this deceptive art. But Jesus came to destroy Satan's lies. He came to free us from those things that retard, distort, and short-circuit everything we are capable of being and doing. He said, "I am come that they might have life, and might have it more abundantly" *(John 10:10)*.

Now, a word to the wise and the strong: John 8:32.

Racism, monopolies, and inappropriate behavior.

Remember what you believe and receive determines how you behave. What I' am about to share with you is *the national plan to empower Black Americans*. It is designed to give you the chance to follow racism to see how far down the rabbit hole it goes, just like in *Alice in Wonderland*:

> Alice: What road do I take?
> Cheshire Cat: Where do you want to go?
> Alice: I don't know!
> Cheshire Cat: Then it doesn't matter which road
> you take!

The Challenges We Face

As the Cheshire Cat said to Alice, who was lost in a wonderland fantasy, it doesn't matter much which road you take if you don't know where you are going. It is time for *Black Americans* to take a good hard look at where they have come from and where they are going.

Are we moving forward or standing still? After centuries of our forefathers' participation in protest marches, *race riots*, and *demonstrations*, and pushing for integration and passage of endless number of civil rights laws, *Black Americans* are increasingly sensing that something is wrong. They question whether or not they are on the right road. A comparative analysis of our *socioeconomic conditions* shows that *Black Americans* have entered the new millennium the same way as they entered the previous four centuries—as impoverished, powerless, and neglected people. Since there have yet to be many programs and public policies specifically offered to eliminate the plight of the Black masses, their future, like their past, looks bleak.

Amidst a rising tide of *White conservatism*, the wealth and income gaps between majority White society and Blacks are widening. Nearly half a century after the supreme court ordered racial desegregation, Black Americans still bear six to eight times their proportional share of poverty, broken homes, homelessness, criminal incarceration, unemployment, and other social pathologies.

Desegregation should have been about redistribution of wealth, power, and resources, not social integration. Social integration has only addressed the symptoms of our dilemma rather than the causes. As indicated, it is extremely difficult for Black people to progress when the same hands that held the whip still hold almost all of the wealth and power.

Abraham Lincoln: White House, slave owner. *Franklin D. Roosevelt:* maldistributed wealth.

During centuries of Black enslavement and *Jim Crow* semi-slavery, the majority of society secured and retained its inherited advantages. While a Black minority inherited a legacy of disadvantages in this race-based society, Whites acquired ownership and control of nearly everything of value as well as a system for keeping Blacks noncompetitive and powerless.

The sheer existence and size of a growing Black underclass is prima facie evidence of institutionalized racism that manipulates symbols, resources, and power to advantage Whites over Blacks. The reality of Black America's dilemma is that they are predestined to become a permanent underclass if they do not break free of the numerous disadvantages they have inherited.

Blacks should get off the social road to nowhere. There are no yellow brick roads to the future, nor will Blacks simply stumble into wealth and power in a competitive society. To find a better road requires *(Jesus)* and Blacks to unlearn old behavior models, strategies, and "learning helplessness" in the race matter. Blacks must understand the nature of the "competitive race" and make a radical metamorphosis. They must decide where they want to go, get out front of their competitors, and work hard to get there first. If Blacks compete, they can expect to succeed and survive in the race for wealth and power.

Race, Racism, and Wealth

Although slavery and *Jim Crow* semi-slavery ended generations ago (so we think), their legacies live on in various forms of *structural racism*. Contrary to popular notions about the concept of race, it is more than a biological grouping. Race is about financial, political, and social currencies. It is a form of stored wealth and power. Whiteness has monetary value. Knowing the origin and nature of the value of the race is essential to any analysis of *Black America's dilemma*. It is important that *Blacks* know why the race problem refuses to die and how it is used to keep them a noncompetitive and powerless group.

The word *race* first appeared with the emergence of the slave practice in the *16th century*. Records indicate the word *race* was selected because the various *European slave-trading nations* were in a contest, competing to profit from the mineral and human wealth of Africa. The *prize* for winning the *race* was the power to develop Western civilization using the wealth extracted out of Africa. Black people were noncompetitors in the *race*. They were the *prizes*, so they could neither *play nor win*. All the competing slave-trading nations, religions, and ethnic groups benefited and were advantaged by *Black slavery.*

Though it took nearly *three hundred years*, and still counting, the concept of race eventually merged with the concept of *biological species.* By that time, *White Europeans* has secured nearly total control of the world's wealth and resource power. Their new concept of *race* established superiority on the basis of who controlled the wealth, power, and resources at that particular time in history. Wealth, power, and privilege became the prerogatives of *nonblacks.*

If Black Americans are to resolve and reverse the legacies of slavery, they must trust *Jesus*, and they must view and treat *racism* based upon its legacies of slavery. They must view and treat *racism* based upon its original meaning and intent. Naturally, those controlling the wealth and power put their cultural values and biological characteristics at the top of the racial order and *Blacks at the bottom.*

Wake up, Black Americans. We are sleeping in dangerous times. Stop talking about *Black lives matter, all lives matter. If Black lives matter,* then why are we destroying one another? Any *Black* man or woman or girl or boy using a *gun* or any sort of weapon to resolve issues are considered a murderer and *a big coward!* You have never learned how to *man up* and take it like a real soldier. Go out like a *Viking* and not like a scary *chump*!

War is not the answer; Jesus is the answer (Acts 4:12, John 3:16). Maybe you are one of those who don't know *Jesus* or don't believe in Him. Maybe you don't even know who you are! Ask yourself the question: *Who am I?*

Who are you?

You will never discover who you are meant to be if you use another person to find yourself. You will never know what you can do by using what other people have done to measure your ability. You will never know why you exist if you use other people's existence to measure it.

All you will see is what they done or who they say they are. If you want to know *who you are*, look at *God!* If you are truly saved by the blood of *Jesus* and you know it, then you know that a part of you is *God's.* The key to understanding life is in the *source of life,* not in life itself.

You are who you are because *God* took you out of Himself. If you want to know who you are, you must look at the *Creator*, not the *creation (Genesis 2:7)*. What I see when I look at you is not all you are. It is only what you have become so far. And that is a child of the King. Your potential is much greater than what you are right now.

What you will become is much more than I or anyone could ever believe now. You are somebody because you came out of *God*, and He leaked some of Himself into you. God pronounces what He sees. You are who *God* says you are, and how you feel or what others say about you is not important. You, again, are who *God* says you are. Your potential is limited only by *God*, not by others.

Many times, *God* is in disagreement with the people closest to you. He may even be in disagreement with you also. Because the only person *God* agrees with is Himself. *God* always sees what men and women only look at. When *God* looks at you, He does not see you. He sees *Christ (Colossians 1:27)*.

God designed you to be somebody special. There's a *book* on you, and some chapters *God* wrote about you haven't even been touched yet. God wants to take you back to the beginning because His plans far outreach your plans. You are somebody simply because you came out of God, and He wants you to become all that He designed you to be and to do.

Who you are depends on what *God* sees. And who you are depends also on what *God* says about what He sees. Who you are is related to where you came from. Don't accept the opinions of others because they do not see what *God* sees. When God looks at you, He sees things that other people ignore.

Always look at the *inventor* and not the *invention*. In other words, never use the creation to find out who you are because the purpose of something is only in the mind of the one who made it. You will never know yourself by relating to the creation—only to the creator.

Many of the *inventions* man has produced would be misunderstood if only the *inventions* were considered and not the *intention* of the *inventor*.

In other words, the man who created the *refrigerator* had in his mind what it was supposed to be used for. He did not intend that it should be used for a trap in the backyard for kids to be locked in and die from suffocation. Even though thousands of children have died in *refrigerators*, that was not the *inventor's* intention. *God* designed you to be somebody. You are fearfully and wonderfully made_(*Psalm 139:14*).

The people who can change the world are the people who have taken *impossible* out of their dictionaries. And also, you have to realize you can do all things through *Christ* who strengthens you. You can do this because the ability of *Christ and His power*, so it is already deposited in you.

Love and prayers always. I'm just a voice.

Why Is There a Universal Hate for God?

In John 15:17, 18, Jesus said to His disciples, "These things I command you, that ye Love one another. If the world hate you, we know that it hated me before it hated you."

In Exodus 20:11–15, it says:

> For in six days the LORD made heaven and earth, the sea, and all that is in them, and rested the seventh day: wherefore the LORD blessed the sabbath day, and hallowed it (*made it holy*)
>
> Honour thy father and thy mother: that thy days may be long upon the land which the Lord thy God giveth thee.
>
> Thou shalt not kill. [See also 1 John 3:14–16 (We know that we have passed from death unto life, because we love the brethren. He that loveth not his brethren abideth in death. Whosoever hateth his brother is a murderer: and ye know that no murderer hath eternal life abiding in him. Hereby perceive we the love of God, because he laid down his life for us: and we ought to lay down our lives for the brethren.)]
>
> Thou shalt not commit adultery.
>
> Thou shalt not steal. [See also Ephesians 4:28 (Let him that stole steal no more: but rather

let him labour, working with his hands the thing
which is good, that he may have to give to him
that needeth.)]

Now all these laws, rules, and regulations come from the *God of the Universe*. Remember that *God is love* (1 John 3:1,11). And if we are made in His image and if we are created in His likeness, why is there so much hate for the God of this Universe. Well, before we get to this point, the answer to the question is *what God?*

There are many *false gods* in this world in which we live in. Many of these gods wants the power, but don't believe in the one with all power *(God's Son, Jesus Christ)*. I believe there are many people living on this earth who don't believe that there is a true and living God. And please understand me that I am not the judge, just a fruit inspector *(Matthew 7:15–16)*. I'm just allowing the word of God to speak to you. In Matthew chapter 24, it deals with *the prophecy of the end.*

And Jesus answered and said, Take heed
that no man deceive you. (Matthew 24:4)

But you must believe in what the Word of God says. Take the time out and read *Matthew 24:4–26*.

Most of the people living on this earth have read *John 3:16*. It speaks of the God that created the heaven and the earth, of how He loved the world so much that He gave His only begotten Son *(Jesus Christ)*. But the key to this verse is the word *believe*. Now, let's proceed with the rest of this verse—that whosoever *believes in Him* shall not perish but have an everlasting life.

Since God loves the world, which includes the entire universe and all that is within it, then why is there is a universal hate for God? If you are sincere and you truly believe in God, then there has to be a thirst for God. You ought to be one that's willing to share God's love to this dying world, but you cannot profess if you don't possess. Now, here is something very important that we all need to know, and that is Satan is the god of this world. It says in *2 Corinthians 4:4*, "In whom the god of this world hath blinded the minds of them which believe not, lest the light of the glorious gospel of Christ, who is the image of God, should shine unto them."

The question I ask myself: How is Satan the god of this world?

Again, I thank God through the Holy Spirit for enlightening me by giving me revelatory knowledge and His wisdom to discern and study His Holy Word. When you look at 2 Corinthians 4:4, the phrase "god of this world" (or "god of this age") indicates that Satan is the major influence on the *ideals, opinions, goals, hopes, and views* of the majority of people. His influence also encompasses the world's *philosophies, education, and commerce.*

The thoughts, ideas, speculations, and false religions of the world are under his control and have sprung from his lies and deceptions. Satan is also called the "prince of the power of the air." In *Ephesians 2:2*, notice that it says he's the prince of the power of the air. It says nothing about him as being the owner and power of the air. He is the "ruler of this world" in *John 12:31*. These titles and many more signify Satan's capabilities. To say, for example, that Satan is the "prince of the power of the air" is to signify that in some way, he rules over the world and the people in it. This is not to say that he rules the world completely; God is still in control of what may seem to be out of control. God is still sovereign. But it does mean that God, in His infinite wisdom, has allowed Satan to operate in this world within the boundaries God has set for him.

When the Bible says Satan has power over the world, we must remember that God has given him domain over unbelievers only.

Believers are no longer under the rule of Satan (*Colossians 1:13*).

Unbelievers, on the other hand, are caught "in the snare of the devil" (*2 Timothy 2:26*), lie in the "power of the evil one" (*1 John 5:19*), and are in bondage to Satan (*Ephesians 2:2*).

So when the Bible says that Satan is the "god of this world," it is not saying that he has ultimate authority. It is conveying the idea that Satan rules over the unbelieving world in a specific way. In 2 Corinthians 4:4, the unbelievers follow Satan's agenda: "The god of this world has blinded the minds of unbelievers, so that they cannot see the light of the gospel of the glory of Christ's love." Satan's scheme includes promoting false philosophies in the world—philosophies that blind *the unbeliever* from the truth of the Gospel. Satan's philosophies are the fortresses in which people are imprisoned, and they must be set free by Christ.

An example of one such false philosophy is the belief that man can earn God's favor by a certain act or acts. Man cannot work to earn God's favor; eternal life is a free gift (*Ephesians 2:8–9*). And that free gift is available through Jesus Christ and in Him alone (*John 3:16, John 14:6*).

You may ask why mankind does not simply receive the free gift of salvation (*John 1:12*). The answer is that Satan, the god of this world, has tempted mankind to follow his pride instead. Satan sets the agenda, the *unbelieving* world follows, and mankind continues to be deceived. It is no wonder that the scripture calls Satan a liar (*John 8:44*) simply because that's *what he does* and that's *who he is*—a liar. This is one of the reasons why there is a hate for God. Mankind has followed Satan for so long until it is just natural for them to hate each other. The *unbelievers* haven't realize that the devil will not go no farther than they carry him, and they don't understand that the only power the devil has is what they give him.

The world of the *unbelievers* hasn't realized that the devil doesn't have the authority nor the power to force them to do or say anything, but he can only suggest. Now, let me get back to explaining this universal hate for God. We're talking about people who just don't believe in the God of this universe, the Creator of all mankind. When you talk to people who are non-Christians today, they are usually very complimentary of Jesus. They'll say, "I don't believe that He was the Messiah, and I don't believe that He was the Son of God, but Jesus was certainly a great person. He was a great teacher. Maybe He was a prophet."

But this kind of high regard for Jesus is, by no means, universal. Even in the Scripture, we find people who reacted to Jesus with hostility, and chief among these people are the scribes and pharisees. We read in *Luke 20* that the scribes and the chief priests sought to have Jesus arrested. In *John 5*, we are told that they wanted to kill Him, and in chapters 8 and 10, they tried to stone Him. When we read these accounts in Scriptures, we are prompted to ask, Why did these people speak the way they did and feel the way they did, with such hostility toward Jesus?

I must admit that hate is running rapidly all over the universe. Look at the kids aged eighteen years and under *committing murder*. Why is this? Well *Proverbs 22:6* is one of the foundational scriptures that many parents are not reading nor are they interested in the Bible itself. If the kids don't obey authority in the home, it's a possibility that they will not obey authority outside the home. Many unsaved parents don't want to have anything to do with the Word of God, so they don't have nothing to lean on. If the foundation be destroyed, what will the righteous do?

This world that we live in is actually in rebellion against the will of God. That's why the Apostle Paul said, *"Be not conformed to this world."* I must say that many are living in this world as if there is no God. They trust in and thing and everybody other than the true and living God. But again the Scripture says in *Psalm 118:8* that it's better to put trust in God than the put confidence in man. Man's social standards falls far short of God's spiritual standards.

That's why James wrote in *chapter 4:4* "that the friendship of the world is enmity [hostile] with God, and whosoever therefore will be a friend of the world is the enemy of God." Why? Because the world's way is in conflict with God's way! In other words, what this world legislates and legitimizes as acceptable behavior for man is often seen as a despicable behavior by the master. And although many people in this world fully believe in a democratic government, there are some shortcomings associated with the democracy. That's why the church of the living God cannot be a democracy. No! The church of the living God is a theocracy! That is, God rules in the church. He established it through His word and through the guidance of the Holy Spirit—what we should do, how we should do it, and when should we do it. Yes, God rules in the church.

The imperfection of a democracy is that its standards and principles are determined not so much by whether they are right or wrong, but rather or not the majority chooses and decides it is acceptable. The decision to legislate and legalize gambling in the form of lottery in Louisiana has nothing to do with right or wrong! But simply more people pull the level (*for*) then (*against*)

The fact that there are areas in this country where it is legal to purchase the sexual services of a woman has nothing to do with rather it is right or wrong, but simply that the majority decides it to be a legitimate transaction. The fact that two men—men!—in the city of San Francisco can apply for and obtain a domestic contract, which equates to a marriage license, does not mean that this activity is right or wrong; it was simply the decision of the majority. There is so much upon which this world puts its seal of approval, which is actually an open rebellion against God's will. So Paul writes, "Don't fit in with the world. Be not conformed to this world."

Anytime you find yourselves coming together to have secular meetings, when governments and legislators and Democrats and Republicans come together, God's name is never mentioned in their conversations. It seems like everything revolves and centers around them; they only have good conversation but no demonstration. We have the Republicans fighting against the Democrats. There's a war going on right here in the USA that no one is concerned about nor paying attention to. We talk about our rights—what rights? Rights to purchase guns with no problem, then we hear on the news that some young kids have killed a bunch of people for what reason. We talk about guns and violence, but we fail to realize that guns don't kill—people kill. We are putting guns in the hands of the wrong people. We never pay mind to what God's Word has to say about all this killing: *Thou shall not kill.* Those who do not believe in God will not apply to His word.

This is another reason why there is a universal hate for God. We lean to our own understanding instead of getting to know the one that created us all and leaning on Him. Just look at this entire universe: it is perishing. The government has failed us, and even the so-called lawmakers have tremendously failed us. No one seems to care. And we have the nerves to label this country the United States of America. It is more divided than it is united.

Satan is the prince of the world (*John 12:31*), and everyone who follows him is under his control.

It's no doubt in my mind that this world is living in a state of confusion—anytime, we call right wrong, and wrong right. We are living in the last days. It's not about *love* anymore. It's not about *loyalty*. It's not about *honesty* anymore. It's all about *me, myself, and I*. Another reason why there's a universal hate for God: look at how this country handles *the homeless people.* No compassion, no concern, *no love.* What is the purpose of all these people that we put in office for? Our elderly is suffering because of a lack of Medicare benefits. Who is stepping up to provide for the elderly?

We have to put our difference on the side and come together to help all that is in need of help. I pray every day that the Lord will remove all of the wicked and evil ones out of the way and replace them with those who have the mind of Christ and a heart for God and a thirst for God and His people. Now, at this moment, I ask you not to hate me. I'm only doing my job, and what I am doing is not designed to upset you. It is to inspire you and encourage you to not be one of those who is a *hater*, but a lover of God and His people.

Those who believe in the Word of God can remember very well how *Cain killed his brother Abel.*

> Cain brought of the fruit of the ground an offering unto the Lord. And Abel he also brought of the firstlings of his flock and of the fat thereof.
>
> And the LORD respected unto *Abel* and to his offering
>
> But unto *Cain* and to his offering, he had no respect. And *Cain* was very wroth and his countenance fallen.
>
> And Cain talked with Abel his brother: and it came to pass, when they were in the field, that Cain rose up against Abel his brother, and slew him [killed]
>
> And the LORD said unto Cain, Where is Abel thy brother? And he said, I know not: Am I my brother's keeper?

And he said, what hast thou done? the voice
of thy brother's blood crieth unto me from the
ground. (*Genesis 4:3–5, 8–10*)

This is one of the first murders that has taken place in the Bible. It appears that if anyone has had an opportunity to read *Genesis 4:1–10*, I can't help but believe that we have a lot of *Cains* living on earth today, who are followers of *Cain in the Bible*. It is very strange how God wrote the *10 Commandment* on stones and one in man's heart, and that is for us to *love one another*.

Love is, and has always been, the love of God. Love was the reason God created us all. And His love is not prejudice, nor there's any racism in the love of God. God created us to love one another, help one another, feed one another, forgive one another, and most of all, God intended for us to live with one another. This was in the back of His mind way before the foundation of the world—that we should be holy and without blame before Him in love. It was God's intention from the start.

God wants everybody to be saved that's why He sent His Son, Jesus Christ, to die for the sins of the whole world, including those who don't believe in Him. My prayer is that the people of this world who do not believe on Jesus will make it their business to confess Him today, right now, before it's too late. Time is running out. God is not willing that any should perish, but that all should come to repentance (*2 Peter 3:9*).

Why Does the World Hate God?

Why does the world hate God? Because they do. Not everyone in the world, but the world definitely *hates God.* There is a hatred of God that is visceral, primeval, strange, and completely irrational.

There is one commandment—and it is really easy to overlook this, not that you don't remember it, but you need to grasp the significance of this statement in the commandment—that says, "You shall not make any graven image, or any likeness of anything that is in heaven above, or that is in the earth beneath, or that is in the water under the earth."

Is this familiar? It is the graven image commandment, and it is in *Exodus 20 verse 4.* Now, continuing in *verse 5,* it says, "You shall not bow down yourself to them, nor serve them, for I the Lord your God am a jealous God, visiting the iniquity of the fathers upon the children unto the third and fourth generation of them that hate me."

A Serious Hatred of God

"That hate me." We are not talking about ignorant people making mistakes and not realizing what they have done. We are talking about a visceral, unreasonable, crude, emotional hatred of God that does exist in the world, and we see examples of it around us all the time. We oftentimes don't realize what it is that we are seeing, but it's there.

God is going to reap His vengeance upon those people who hate Him. Now, guess why it is the third and fourth generation. Do you have a clue on that? Is that fair?

Well, actually God said, "It is to the third and fourth generation of them that hate me," which I presume that if the fourth generation does not hate God, then He is not going to bring vengeance on them, right? But have you seen what is happening in the Middle East—in Palestine? How many generations would it take to breed the hatred out of all the Palestinian people for the Jews? Hatred of the Jews is taught in the schools; it is taught on their television and all over the Middle East. I mean, how many generations among Arabs would it take to get rid of the hatred for Jews?

People who hate God teach their children to hate God, and so on, it goes, and consequently, this type of thing goes on generation after generation. And there it is, right there in black and white, in your Bible. There are people who hate God. They want all mention of God expunged from public life. They now have the Ten Commandments removed from many courtrooms. Those people have an irrational desire to get rid of that symbol of God

People who hate God have fought prayer of any kind in school, and even a moment of silence is troubling because it implies prayer. And there are people who don't want that moment of silence in school so that the kids can have a moment to reflect and bow their heads to pray before an exam or before they go to class because it might imply prayer. We definitely need prayers today.

A Bible in the Classroom

Battles have been fought in the school for just the presence of a Bible. A teacher has been threatened and not allowed to have his personal Bible on his desk in his classroom, and he might have lost his job. This was such a threat that some people have gone to court to get rid of this Bible on his desk, and he would probably have lost his job if he has not taken it out of his classroom.

Now, not everyone who participates in these efforts hates God. I do not mean to imply that by any stretch of the imagination.

Useful, Selfish People

They were the people who had these great ideas, these lofty and grandeur notions of what society could be like and ought to be like and how they could overcome the problems of man by man. In other words, it is a humanistic thing. They plant their faith in what man can do instead of having their faith in what God can do.

I'll tell you something. One of the most dangerous ideas ever to be on this planet is *utopianism*, the idea that we are going to perfect human beings to create a perfect society without God. It is one of the most dangerous ideas subverting human liberty and human freedom that has ever come down.

Right now, there are people who *hate God,* and there are "useful people" who help them. There are people who are well-intentioned, and they don't realize the implications of what they're doing or why it's happening.

There's a War Going On

There is a war going on. It is a war that has been going on for generation after generation after generation, and frankly, ever since Adam and Eve were thrusted out the Garden of Eden. Paul spoke of it and acknowledged that there was a war when he wrote *2 Corinthians chapter 10.*

In *verses 3–5,* Paul had this to say, "For though we live in the world, we do not wage war as the world does. The weapons we fight with are not the weapons of the world. [The King James Version says, "The weapons of our warfare are not carnal, on the contrary they have divine power to demolish strongholds."] We demolish arguments and every pretension that sets itself up against the knowledge of God, and we take captive every thought to make it obedient to Christ." Now, the King James Version is more accurate in one part of this. It says, "The weapons of our warfare are not carnal." The word *carnal* in verse 4 in the Greek is *sarkikos,* and it means "of the flesh."

Pretension against the Knowledge of God

There are constitutional arguments out there today that are against God, and this is what Paul called in *2 Corinthians 10 verse 5* "a pretension that sets itself up against the knowledge of God."

The fact of the matter is that most of what's going on out there right now is pure pretense. It isn't a question of usurpation of people's liberties. For the fact is what possible harm could there be having a monument, a statue of sculpture, which has the Ten Commandments on it on public property or in a courtroom?

You could have put a statue of Eros, the Greek god of love there, and that would have been just fine. Nobody would have sued, nobody would have raised Cain over it on that issue unless some Christians decide that it is pagan, and we can't have that. But I have my questions whether the courts would have paid any attention to it or not. But put the Ten Commandments there! What is the problem with this? It should be easy. The seventh commandment is "Thou shalt not commit adultery." Right? We don't want that in there. Sexual sin is the defining characteristic of this generation.

Every generation has it's defining sin, and sexual sin is the defining characteristic of our generation in our country.

To have the Ten Commandments on public property or on a courtroom also identifies God with the fourth commandment: "Remember the Sabbath day to keep it holy." And if you read your Bible, you would realize that when you get to *Exodus 31 verse 13*, it talks about God who says, "My Sabbaths you shall keep: for it is a sign between me and you throughout your generations; that you may know that I am Jehovah that does sanctify you and sets you apart."

In other words, the Sabbath is the thing that identifies God by name. It's who God is. To say that our country was founded on an idea of some generic god is almost blasphemous. Now, you may want to speak of a generic word for God, but there is no such thing as a generic god.

God Is the Creator of This Entire Universe

God is the creator. He made it all, with the earth that we stand on, the air that we breathe, and everything else. He made it. Now, we're talking about the Creator.

Now, my question is, Are these Ten Commandments identifying that creator? Sure, they do! Sure, they do! And that poses a problem. Now, probably the most important is that commandment that is read to you today.

We Must Not Serve Other Gods

"You shall not make any graven image, or any likeness of anything that is in heaven above, or in the earth beneath or in the water under the earth. You shall not bow yourself down to them, nor serve them."

Did you notice that? It is not merely a question of bowing down to them; you are not to do that, "neither are you to serve them, for I the Lord your God am a jealous God, visiting the iniquity of the fathers upon the children to the third and fourth generation of them that hate me" *(Exodus 20:5)*.

Now, this commandment is about a lot more than pictures on the wall or icons in a Greek church or statues in a Roman Catholic Church.

It's about the rejection of God for an idol. It is about the *hatred of God* because that's what the commandment says it's about. It's about people who will turn their back on God, who know who He is and who reject Him out of hand.

Psalm 81 verses 7–9 says, "In your distress you called and I rescued you, I answered you out of the thundercloud. I tested you at the waters of Meribah. Hear, O my people, and I will warn you, if you will just listen to me, O Israel! You shall have no foreign god among you, you shall not bow down to an alien god."

Now, remember that bowing down to a foreign god is an issue connected with the hatred of God.

> "I am the Lord your God that brought you out of Egypt. Open wide your mouth and I will fill it.
>
> But my people will not listen to me; Israel would not submit to me,
>
> So I gave them over to the stubborn hearts to follow their own devices.
>
> "If my people would but listen to me, if Israel would follow my ways." Just listen to me and follow my ways,
>
> "How quickly would I subdue their enemies and turn my hand against their foes!
>
> Those who hate the LORD would cringe before him, and their punishment would last forever,
>
> But you would be fed with the finest of wheat, and with honey from the rock. I would satisfy you." (Psalm 81:10–16)

The Hebrew word *sane,* which is translated *hate,* is a very strong word in Hebrew, and it means to hate personally. You are not talking about a dislike; it is talking about a personal, direct hatred toward an individual. And here, He's talking about people who are enemies of God, *who hate God.*

He says, "If my people would just listen to me, if they would just pay attention. If they would just do what I tell them to do," and the things that God tells us to do are not hard. They are not to climb every mountain. They are things like if you are called to serve on a jury. When you go in and sit on a jury, then render honest judgment. Don't let yourself be influenced by how much money people have or how much they don't have. Be honest. Don't take money unjustly from one person to give it to another in a lawsuit. Don't unjustly send a man to prison. Judge honest judgment. Treat your neighbor right.

Hear the cause of the widow. Feed the hungry. Give your clothes to people who don't have things to wear.

These are simple, down-to-earth good things that we are supposed to do to one another that God expects of us. God says, "You will not do those things." If we would just do what He tells us to do, then our enemies and the enemies of God would cringe at that.

You can see hints about that in today's news, can't you? You can see hints of it whenever someone stands up for God, whenever someone stands up for what is right, and whenever someone starts to talk about the eternal creator God, the demands He makes, and His expectations for man, God's enemies cringe, and they hate it. And they hate these people just like they *hate God.*

The Men of God Are Hated

There's a man in the Bible, and his name is Stephen. He is a man that you may have heard about if you have ever read the book of Acts. He's a dominant figure there, but he did not last very long because he told the truth and spoke the truth in power. You will find the story in the seventh chapter of Acts. I think it is very interesting.

Stephen was speaking to the Jews around him, and he's been extremely effective in arguing the case for Christianity among Jews, says in verses 51–52: "You stiffnecked people, with uncircumcised hearts and ears! You are just like your fathers. You always resist the Holy Spirit! Was there ever a prophet your fathers did not persecute?"

What a thing to say! Here are all these Jews in front of him and he says, "Was there ever a prophet that your fathers did not persecute?" Why? Well, we will come to it later, but Jesus told His disciples, "If they hated me, they are going to hate you" (John 15:18).

Every single man to whom God spoke of old and every single man that He gave a vision and a message to, He told them, "You go and tell them what I want you to tell them." Every single one of *those men was hated for it.*

Jeremiah was actually put in a cesspool up to his armpits and left there to die. He didn't die; they pulled him out later, but that was the intent of the people who put him there. They hated him. Why did they hate him?

Here's a question that has always bothered me about things like this. Why is it that whenever you hear an idiot standing up and saying bad things, you can shrug your shoulders, walk around, and say, "Oh well, there's another one coming around next week if this one doesn't do the trick. It is just one after the other." Why is it that we can't just turn our back on these people? You might walk out tonight and see someone on the street corner with a sign that says, "Flee from the wrath to come." Does he worry you? Does he bother you? No.

Why were the Jews so bothered with this? Because it was true. That's why they were bothered by it. They would not have been bothered by it otherwise.

Well, this is what happened to Stephen. He said in *Acts 7 verses 52–53*, "Was there ever a prophet your fathers did not persecute? They even killed those who predicted the coming of the Righteous One. And now you have betrayed and murdered him. You who have received the law that was put into effect through angels but have not obeyed it."

Now, would that really have bothered you that much if you had obeyed it? Hardly! Probably not!

Continuing in verses 54–58, "When they heard this, they were furious and gnashed their teeth at him. But Stephen, full of the Holy Spirit, looked up to heaven and saw the glory of God, and Jesus standing at the right hand of God. "Look," he said, "I see heaven open and the Son of Man standing at the right hand of God." At this they covered their ears and, yelling at the top of their voices, they all rushed at him, dragged him out of the city and began to stone him."

If I was talking to some guy and he was giving me a bad time and I rejected what he was saying and he looked up and said, "Oh, oh, I see Jesus standing at the right hand of God in heaven." What would my reaction be? Well, I would probably think that he was crazy. And depending on how dangerous he might seem to be to the people around him, I might call someone to restrain him, but probably not. I probably would just turn and walk away.

These Jews didn't walk away from Stephen. They were so angry. The King James version says, "They gnashed on him with their teeth." I don't think they bit him. The NIV says that they "gnashed their teeth at him." They were so furious with him they almost bit their tongue off. Why? *Because they hated God.* Initially, it was a question of Stephen, *but they hated God.* And because they are among those *people in the world who hate God* and would never admit that they do, they hated the man whom God had sent. Why this visceral hatred of this good man? People don't reserve this kind of hatred for fools. They reserve it for people when they feel threatened in their innermost being. They are afraid. It takes fear to generate this kind of hatred and this kind of anger. For people who are not afraid, don't get mad. There's no particular reason to do so.

Another Reason Jesus Is Hated

Here's Jesus, one day, and the story is in *Mark chapter 3 verses 1–2,* which says, "Jesus went into the synagogue, [it was a Sabbath] and there was a man there that had a withered hand, and they watched him, whether he would heal him on the Sabbath day, that they might accuse him."

Now, I have to tell you, this is one of those things that, every time I read it, I shake my head and look to heaven. I can't understand this. Here is a man who walks into the synagogue, and there is a possibility that Jesus might heal the withered hand of this man and some Jews were watching to see if He will do it today. And He shouldn't do it today because it is the Sabbath day. Where does this kind of thinking come from? Well, I know the answer to that question.

In *Mark 3:4–5,* Jesus asked them, "Is it lawful to do good on the Sabbath days, or to do evil? To save life, or to kill?" No one answered him. They would not even have a discussion with Jesus about the merits of His case. They wouldn't dispute with Him and wouldn't argue with Him. They didn't even answer him. And when He had looked around upon them and He was angry, being grieved for the hardness of their hearts, He said to the man, "Stretch forth your hand."

I almost wish I could have been there to see that miracle. Miracles are usually much more subtle than that. But to be able to see this poor guy with a withered hand and his arm held against his chest. Now, Jesus didn't do anything. There was no work involved. Jesus just said, "Stretch your hand out!" And the man stretched his hand out, and it became whole just like the other one.

This would have been such an incredible thing to see with your own eyes, and it says in *verse 6*, "The Pharisees went out and immediately took counsel with the Herodians against him, on how they might destroy him."

Now, that is hard to figure, but if you can't sit back in your chair sometimes and think about this for a little while and answer this question, then you are not studying your Bible seriously enough because this is an important question. This is a good man. A charismatic man. A wonderful teacher, who had the power to make blind men see, who caused cripples to walk, who could do all these wonderful things, and could heal this man with a withered hand, and they wanted to destroy Him. You have to find a way in your mind to understand what's going on here because it's important. If you can't understand this, you cannot understand anything about the spiritual warfare that is going on in the world right now because the same spirit that was in that synagogue on that day is here right now. The same spirit.

Why the Jews Wanted to Kill Jesus?

So let's understand what's going on. The Jews wanted to kill Jesus. Here is the way Luke tells the story, in *chapter 6 verses 10–11*, "Jesus, looking around at them all, said to the man, "Stretch forth your hand." And he did so, and his hand was restored whole as the other. And they were filled with madness."

They were filled with madness—an insane stupid rage, an irrational rage is what it was. I think the Greek word *anoia* even implies that ignorant, stupid, irrational quality to the anger. It was a madness. It was not a reasoned anger. Jesus was angry because of the hardness of their heart. It was clear, and it was reasoned. It was right. Their anger was totally unreasonable. It was madness.

For My Love, They Hated Me

Psalm 109:1–3 says, "Hold not your peace, O God of my praise; For the mouth of the wicked and the mouth of the deceitful are open against me. They have spoken against me with a lying tongue. They compass me about with words of hatred and they fought against me without a cause."

You know, it doesn't take a lot of theology here to all of a sudden realize that you have fallen back into a prophecy of Christ—a prophecy of the one who was to come in the name of God and as the Son of God, doing the things that Jesus did. This prophet years before said, "They have spoken against me with a lying tongue." Why did they lie about Jesus? Why were they willing to put out good money to hire witnesses to tell false things about him? Why would they do that?

Continuing in verse 4, "They compassed me about also with words of hatred; and fought against me without a reason to do so."

David then says this in verses 4–5, "For my love they are my adversaries, but I give myself to prayer. They have rewarded me evil for good, and hatred for my love."

How bad is this? How awful is this? "That for my love, they are my adversaries." It is not for my evil works. It isn't because I hurt them. It is for my love. Who had Jesus harmed? Who had He hurt? What man had He struck? Had He, in anyway, taken anything from another? A shoe latchet? A coin? A thread? A garment? What had Jesus done to hurt or harm or take away from anyone?

"For my love they are my adversaries." It was for Jesus's love that they hated Him. "They have rewarded me evil for good, and hatred for my love."

Then here is what Jesus says about people who do this sort of thing. I think we should stop for a moment and think very carefully about what He says here.

Verses 6–12 of Psalms 109 says:

> Set a wicked man over him. Let Satan stand at his right hand.
>
> When he is judged, let him be condemned, let his prayer become sin.
>
> Let his days be few, and let another take his office. [Reference is Judas Iscariot.]
>
> Let his children be fatherless, and let his wife be a widow,
>
> Let his children be continuing vagabonds and beg, let them seek their bread out of the desolate places.
>
> Let the extortioner catch all that he has; and let the strangers spoil his labor.
>
> Let there be no one to extend mercy to him: neither let there be any to favor his fatherless children.

This is awful! Do you know why? It is because of hatred. What father will not pass on some of his hatred to his children? You need to think about that you, young moms and dads. Your attitudes, your hatred, your visceral dislikes of some people, and so forth are going to get passed on to your children.

> Let his posterity be cut off; and in the generation following let their name be blotted out.
>
> Let the iniquity of his fathers be remembered with the Lord; and let not the sin of his mother be blotted out.
>
> Let them be before the Lord continually, that he may cut off the memory of them from the earth. (Psalms 109:13–15)

Wow, that is serious. But why?

> Because he remembered not to show mercy, but persecuted the poor and the needy man, that he might even slay the broken in heart.
>
> As he loved cursing, so let it come unto him: as he delighted not in blessing, so let it be far from him.
>
> As he clothed himself with cursing like as with his garment, so let it come into his bowels like water, and like oil into his bones.
>
> Let it be to him as the garment which covers him, and for a girdle wherewith he is girded continually.
>
> Let this be the reward of mine adversaries from the LORD, and of them that speak evil against my soul." (Psalms 109:16–20)

I would think one would want to be very, very careful about speaking evil of good people, by cutting down good men, and about not showing respect that we should for people who are doing good works because, after all, "No one can do a good work in Jesus's name. He said can speak lightly of me."

> But you, O Sovereign LORD, deal well with me for your name's sake; out of the goodness of your love, deliver me. (Psalms 109:21)

Jesus Resurrected Lazarus

There is a story in the New Testament, John 11, in the ministry of Jesus that I always find fascinating. Lazarus was sick, and word came to Jesus that Lazarus was sick, and Jesus knew what he was going to do. He waited. He waited until Lazarus was dead. He was going to go there and raise him from the dead. He was going to wait four days because He wanted everybody to be sure they knew and understood and believed that Lazarus really was dead.

People at that time believed that the soul of a man might hang around the body and might come back into the body, and the person might come back to life. Why would they think that? Because people had come out of comas, whom they thought were dead, had sat up and walked out of the room. So the whole idea was to wait because in three days, they would know. So Jesus waited for four days so that everyone would be sure to understand what it was that He was about to do.

Jesus came there and all the people were crying, weeping, wailing, and moaning, and Mary came out and said, "Lord, if you had been here, my brother would not have died" (John 11:42)

And Jesus was really hurting inside because of the death of his friend, and he went up to the tomb, and it tells us in verses 43–44: "He spoke and He cried with a loud voice, 'Lazarus, come out!' And he that was dead came walking out, struggling with his grave clothes. His face was still bound with the napkin and he could hardly find his way out of the tomb."

Lazarus was a man who was dead. Nobody could doubt that he was dead. Mary even thought he would be stinking by now, but he was alive.

Now, let's notice verses 46–58. It says, "But some of them went their way to the Pharisees, and told them what Jesus had done. Then gathered the chief priests and Pharisees, a council, and said, 'What are we going to do? This man is doing many miracles. If we let him alone all men will believe on him.'"

What's wrong with that? Up to that point, not much.

Then they said, "The Romans shall come and take away both our place and our nation."

Our place, they will take it away, and we will be out of office. We will be powerless, and we will lose everything we have got. We will lose our authority over the people. They have told us now, in no uncertain terms. Precisely, what it is that bothers them?

Why Were the Jews Afraid of Jesus?

The Jews were afraid of Jesus. They were scared to death of this mild man, who wouldn't hurt a flea. The fact that Jesus was gentle was a given fact, and they were so afraid of this man because they were afraid that people would believe Him, that the people would follow Him, that they would lose their following, and that they would lose their authority. They would lose the respect that people had for them. It was all about themselves, and they were deathly afraid of Christ.

"Then from that day forward," it says in John 11 verse 53, "they took counsel to put him to death."

Now, it would be one thing if you and I could stand aside from all of this and just watch all these things going by us in the world— all of this hatred of God. If we could only be spectators, but we can't. We must let the world see the love of God in us, even if we have to suffer. Remember, *following Christ comes with a price.*

We Are Commanded to Love One Another (John 14:15)

Jesus said, in John 15:1–5, one of the greatest messages of His life and one of His last. He said:

> "I am the true vine, and my Father is the husbandman. Every branch in me that bears not fruit he takes away, every branch that bears fruit, he prunes and so it can bring forth much fruit. Now you are clean through the word that I have spoken to you. Stay in me, and I in you. The branch cannot bear fruit of itself, except it stay in the vine; no more can you, except you abide in me. I am the vine, you are the branches: He that abides in me, and I in him, the same brings forth much fruit: because without me you can't do nothing."

He goes on to say, "If you abide in me, and my words abide in you, you shall ask what you will, and it will be done" (John 15:7).

That's a tremendous promise. What we may often overlook with that though is it demands the same kind of response from us because it's a covenantal type of promise. "If I am willing to do whatever you ask of me, you have to be ready to do whatever I ask of you. Now, what I am going to ask of you may not be comfortable for you." Jesus has made that as clear as He could to His disciples.

Now, He goes on to try to explain to them what it is that is coming.

> "As my Father has loved me, so I have loved you, stay in my love. If you keep my commandments you shall abide in my love, just as I have kept my Father's commandments, I abide in his love. These things have I spoken to you that my joy might remain in you and your joy might be full. This is my commandment, that you love one another as I have loved you." (John 15:9–12)

Okay, people, that's the problem that you and I have to deal with. Jesus said to us as His disciples that "we are to love one another just like He loved us."

> Greater love has no man than this, that a man lay down his life for his friends. You are my friends if you do whatever I command you. Henceforth I call you not servants; for the servant doesn't know what his lord does: but I have called you friends; everything that I have heard of my Father I have made known to you. You have not chosen me, but I have chosen you, and ordained you, that you should go and bring forth fruit, and that your fruit should last: that whatsoever you ask of the Father in my name, he may give it to you. (John 15:13–16)

Then He says this in verse 18, "If the world hates you, know this, it hated me before it hated you."

The People of This World Will Hate You

Just make up your mind to this. Jesus said in John 15 verse 19, "If you were of the world, the world would love his own: but because you are not of the world, but I have chosen you out of the world, the world is going to hate you."

They hated Jesus, and they're going to hate us. We should not do anything to make them hate us, except for the fact that loving them sometimes can cause them to hate you all the more.

Verse 20 says, "Remember the word I said to you, "The servant is not greater than his lord. If they have persecuted me, they will also persecute you. If they have kept my word, they will keep your word."

There are two classes of people in this world. There are people who will keep God's word, and there are people who hate it. And if you are a bearer of God's word, if you are a bearer of His truth, and if you are bearer of Him, then they are going to hate you just like they hated Him *(John 15:18)*

> All these things he said they will do to you
> for my name's sake, because they don't know him
> that sent me. If I had not come and spoken to
> them, they would not be guilty of sin. but now
> they have no cloak or excuse for their sin. He that
> hates me, hates my Father also (John 15:21–23)

Of course, of course, for if you have seen Jesus, you have seen the Father. You can't imagine you are going to hate Jesus and love the Father. Impossible.

> If I had not done among them the works
> which no one else did, they would have no sin;
> but now they have seen and also hated both me
> and my Father.

When this came to pass, that the word might be fulfilled that is written in their law, They hated me without a cause.

But when the Comforter is come, whom I will send from the Father, even the Spirit of truth, which proceeds from the Father, he will testify of me:

And you will bear witness, because you have been with me from the beginning. (John 15:24–27)

What really caught my attention is in verse 27 because He didn't say, *"You should bear witness."* He said, *"You will."* One way or the other, you will.

John chapter 16, verses 1–2, Jesus says, "These things I have spoken to you, that you should not be offended. They will put you out of the synagogues, yeah the time comes, and that whoever kills you will think he does God a service."

He is not talking about *secular government.* He's talking about *religious people.* Notice that I said religious people.

The time will come when they will kill you, and they will think they do God a service and "They will do it because they have not known the Father and they have not known me" (John 16:3).

Remember the movie *The Passion of Christ*?

You may have heard of the movie *The Passion* by Mel Gibson. It created a lot of opposition from people who had never seen the movie than I think any movie in the history of moviemaking. It is a movie about the last twelve hours leading up to Jesus's death on the stake. It is vivid and crystal clear. All of the language in the movie had been done in Aramaic and Latin, the languages of the time. If you have seen this movie, you will not understand a word that is spoken but will understand everything that is taking place on the screen. Mel Gibson is telling the story visually, not so much orally.

This movie is the story of man's hatred for God, everything about God, God's love for man, and God's ultimate sacrifice for man in the face of man's hatred. In fact, this story is the climax of man's hatred for God.

In many ways, when Jesus said, "Our Father, forgive them for they do not know what they do," it spoke across a broad spectrum of mankind with a great deal of hope because even the people who hated Him really did not understand the genesis of their hatred. They did not understand where it was coming from. They did not understand when it was born. They did not understand where it was taking them. I think even those people are included when Jesus said, "Father, forgive them for they don't have a clue."

And so, living in the world we live in today, I think you need to be very sensitive to the fact that the world hates God. It is not new. It is as old as man and has been around for so long that nobody remembers the genesis of it, but you see it. You see it in the evening news. You'll see it in your schools. You'll see it on the street. You'll see it all over the place. Don't be dismayed; you are going to have to live in the world, but Jesus said, "I have overcome the world" (John 16:33).

The time will come when men will learn better than that, but between here and there, be really careful that you never wind up being a useful idiot for those who hate God.

We've Become a Country of Hate, Disrespect, and Unforgiveness

We've become a country of blame and finger-pointing.

We've become a country of entitlement.

We've become a country that is all about *me*, not about *we*.

We've become a country that's led to believe we must pick a side (and that anyone who disagrees with us is wrong).

We've become a country where morals have been thrown out the window. Where good teachings in the home is not applied anymore.

What we're witnessing today in American society disgusts me. In fact, I'm displeased at all points with all the hate, one-for-another-sidedness, and a complete lack of respect for others.

So I wanted to share facts and realities that will bring some attention to the real problem in this universal hate for God.

First, Here's What Is Not the Core Problem

The problem is *not* politicians (there have been both good and bad politicians for thousands of years—nothing new here).

The problem is *not* the media (media can only amplify the voices, behaviors, and morals of the society that it reports on—they are not the problem, the people are).

The problem is *not* income inequality (this, too, has been around for thousands of years; my guess is that there will always be large differences in income, provided some people work harder, smarter, and take bigger risks than others).

The problem is *not* the police. (For anyone who believes police are the issue, have you ever considered why they have a job in the first place? It's to protect law-abiding citizens from the knuckleheads who refuse to obey the law; if you want to disband the police, simply stop breaking the law, and they won't have a job.)

The problem is *not* racism (racism and discrimination have been going on for thousands of years—from race to religion, it's not new; and even if racism ends tomorrow, it still doesn't fix the fundamental problems in this world).

Here's the Real Problem in This Universe

The real problem can all be summed up in one: *no God, no love.* (It all starts in the *home.*)

"No society has ever survived after its family life deteriorated."

Yes, the real reason we have so much hate and dysfunction in this universe is that we've ripped apart and bastardized the one thing that holds any society together—*God, love, and family.*

Why is family so important?

Family is where you learn right from wrong.

Family is where you first learn to play together as a team.

Family is where you learn how to have healthy conversations and debates. *And most definitely forgiveness.*

Family is where you learn that it's okay to still love someone even if you don't completely agree with them.

Family is where you learn it's *not* okay to discriminate, that it's *not* okay to treat others badly, and that it's *not* okay to tease someone because they look different than you (regardless if it's color of skin, if they're handicapped, the way they dress, etc.).

Family is where you learn that you aren't entitled to anything, that you've got to put in the *work* for anything you want or desire.

Family is where you learn that you can't be selfish—that it's *not* all about you, it's about the family unit. *But number one is God!*

Family is where you learn about *love* and what it looks like to do good in God's eyes.

Yet today, we have hardly any focus on the family—it's no longer a priority.

Today, you're considered weird if your family has sit-down dinners, prays at the table, and has real discussions as a family.

Sadly, it's now easier to disregard our families and blame anything we can point our fingers on as being the problem.

All while we celebrate and applaud the celebrities who cheat on their spouses and leave them for "better-looking" replacements.

We celebrate divorces like they are nothing more than an eighth grader leaving their junior high sweetheart. [Have we completely forgotten that marriage is a covenant that every couple signed with their spouse and God? (Matthew 19:6, Hebrews 13:4)]

What's really sad is that we've forgotten what it means to be loving parents, who are fully engaged with our children. It's easier to just buy them a phone or have them sit in front of the TV than it is to be the loving parents that we know we're called to be, especially when we parent ourselves by the Book (*Bible*). And hardly anyone has time to have a sit-down dinner with our family because we're all too busy. I know the feeling…it's not easy to be a good parent. There are no perfect parents, but if the world has God's love, I'm here to tell you that *it's work!*

Are you convinced that a breakdown of the family is the core issue?

Spend a day at your local prison and ask the prisoners who've committed the worst crimes what their family life was like. Almost every single one of them will tell you they came from a broken and dysfunctional family.

Heck, spend a day at any public school in America and just ask the teachers what the biggest problem is. They'll be quick to tell you that more and more kids lack parents who care, that countless parents are using public schools as daycare so they don't have to put any work into their kids, that the family life in so many of these young children is nonexistent. How sad.

How can we possibly expect anyone to know right from wrong and how to love thy neighbor if we're not doing it as a family?

How can we expect to have a stable foundation as a society if there isn't a stable family structure?

Simply put, a breakdown in the family results in a breakdown in society.

It's really simple math: disrespectful kids with no foundation equal disrespectful adults with no moral compass.

That's always been the case, and there are just more of them today than at any time in the universe of American history.

Why Is There So Much Killing and Injustice in This Universe?

We Must Share God's Love

Have you ever wondered what is going on with the world and why there is a sudden surge in violence, murder, and senseless killing?

I wasn't surprised with God's response to me when I asked this question. This is what I heard: *"All you need is love!"* To have love, you first need to have God (*1 John 4:7–21, John 13:34–35*).

I know this sounds cliché (and it is also the title to a Beatles song), but I feel a seriousness from the Lord. I would like to share more of the prophetic insight that I received and also present a solution.

There is a time of shaking.

We are in a time of shaking as God is preparing us for a coming revival. Naturally, the enemy does not want this revival to happen. Everywhere you look, people seem to be in fear. Terrorism itself inflicts fear upon people, and it can get us out of God's perfect peace.

I was reading a statistic by the CDC (Center for Disease Control) that the leading cause of death in the United States is heart failure. This reminded me of what Jesus said: "Men's hearts failing them from fear and the expectation of those things which are coming on the earth, for the powers of the heavens will be shaken" (Luke 21:26 NKJV)

It is interesting that Jesus said people would suffer from heart failure due to fear. We are seeing this happen right now. It is important to remove fear from our lives and instead be filled with the Holy Spirit and faith, hope, and love (1 Corinthians 13:13).

For God has not given us a spirit of fear, but power and love and of a sound mind (2 Timothy 1:7 NKJV).

As we cast out fear and replace it with love, we will receive a sound mind. Many people are suffering from mental illness, causing them to act out in violence. This is from a lack of love and allowing fear to overpower us.

Jesus said to love, *not hate*.

Jesus said the most important commandments were to love God, our neighbors, and ourselves (Mark 12:28–31).

As I look around, I see that these verses have not been valued to the level that Jesus asked us. Just look at social media, and you will agree with me. When we begin to judge others and step out of perfect love, we invite fear into our lives.

Here's the most powerful revelation we can have on this and the solution as well: There is no fear in love; but perfect love casts out fear because fear involves torment. But he who fears has not been made perfect in love (1 John 4:18 NKJV)

We need to get into the perfect love that John (and Jesus) talked about. As we step into perfect love, we will no longer have fear.

But if we allow fear to rule in our lives, then a tormentor can be assigned to us.

This is the condition of people today. Tormentors are being assigned to people's minds, causing a dark cloud of hatred to cover our land. This is also causing people to engage in senseless killing. Even believers can be tormented by fear and be inflicted with hopelessness in their souls and sickness in their bodies.

What is the solution?

As simple as it sounds, we need to love and not hate or judge others. It is a time like never before to step into God's perfect love.

We can do this by being kind and compassionate to one another. We can turn the dark cloud over our nation into an open heaven of

God's love and light. But it requires us to cast out fear and be filled with the love of Jesus.

When it comes down to it, as God said, "All you need is love!"

Again, I must truly say this with conviction that if the creatures that God has created would read and study God's Word and apply every detail and every truth of it, the people of this world would discover that God is love (1 John 3:1–11, 17. I believe that if every person that's living on God's planet Earth would get to know Jesus and be saved, it would help them to know that if they have Jesus as their Lord and Savior, they would also have His Love. The Bible says, "For this is the message that ye heard from the beginning, that we should love one another." (Also, see John 13:34–35.)

I can recall in God's Word when God have given Moses the Ten Commandments for the children of Israel, they had ten of God's commandments. The question that comes to my mind is, Why did God give the children of Israel the Ten Commandments? Well, I believe He gave them to the children of Israel because He gave them to us to make sure that *we* would also become aware that we could not fulfil them on our own, through our own power, and to make it painfully clear to us that we sin and fall short of the holiness, righteousness, and glory of God (*Romans 3:23*) and, therefore, are in need of a savior.

That is what those Ten Commandments had pointed to. But isn't it perplexing that God has given ten to the children of Israel and one to the people of this universe? And sad to say, most of the people of this world cannot even keep the one commandment that Jesus wrote in man's heart, and that is to love one another.

Jesus Himself declared in His Holy Word according to 2 Timothy 3:1–3: "*This* know also, that in the last days perilous (dangerous) times shall come. For men shall be lovers of their own selves, covetous, boasters, proud, blasphemers, disobedient to parents, unthankful, unholy. Traitors, heady, high-minded, lovers of pleasures more than lovers of God." To be honest, it seems like the friendship of man is greater than the friendship of God. I say this from reading the above verses.

And believe me when I say this: If there's no regard for God, then there definitely won't be any regard for our fellow man on this earth.

Sometimes, the question I ask myself is, "If God had created a world without violence, it also would have been a world without freedom."

God, in His love, gave us the freedom to choose. Our freedom has brought about a lot of the suffering apparent in the world.

God is personally involved in the affairs of the world. He entered this world as a human person and allowed himself to experience pain and suffering right along with us. His plan, however, is to heal the world one day, for good, to take away all hatred and violence. Ultimately, we don't know why there is hatred and violence, but isn't it better to go through life with God than without Him?

Jesus would give an answer like the story of the Good Samaritan. "Love your neighbor as yourself." The man answers, "Who is my neighbor?"

The problem is that many people are selfish, and they only think about themselves. We try to define what we think is good, and we choose what is best for us, not our neighbors. We don't love our neighbors well like God has commanded us to do.

God is not a mean person; God is love. God is aware, and He cares. God takes all of the pain on Himself and feels it all very deeply. He also offers solutions to the brokenness instead of turning his back on it. But still, the question remains: Why is there a universal hate for God?

The part that really speaks to this question is when talking about relationships. God created us out of love to be in harmony with Himself, with each other, and with the world around us. But many people have been separated from God, destroyed relationships with each other, and don't live in harmony with the world because of their selfishness and brokenness. My wife for forty-one years plus often asks the question "Why doesn't everybody love one another?" She always says I which that everybody would get alone with each other and be on speaking terms with one another.

And this is our prayer that we both pray every Monday, at one o'clock. We pray for this entire universe and every individual that is living in it. That God's amazing love would touch the heart of every living creature that God has created on this earth.

Even in our homes, our schools, our churches, and on our jobs, God's love should always be seen in His children *(the redeemed)*. Just to be clear on this: If anyone ought to sense the love of God, it should be when forks come into the house of the Lord. Why? Because love is the establishment of the church.

The world needs to know that Jesus Christ demonstrated His love toward us all, and that while we were yet sinners, Christ died for us *(Romans 5:8)*. Jesus just didn't have conversation; he also had demonstration. He showed the entire world of how much He loved us *(John 3:16–17)*. God so love the world, not hate the world. He loves the sinners, but He hates the sin. That was why God gave his only Son so that those who believe in him should not perish, but should have an eternal life in Jesus Christ. He loved the world so much that He was willing to die for it.

Just imagine, if everybody on this earth believed in Jesus Christ and are saved from the penalty of their sins, there wouldn't be a need for guns, weapons, hate for police officers, crimes, rapes, robbery, liars, thieves, and homongers—no violence, no dislike, no racism, etc. But as Christians, we must continue to be in prayer on behalf of a world that is dying without Christ.

We much continue to push—*pray, until something happens.*

We don't have the power to change the people; that's in God's hand. All we can do is love everybody even when they don't love us back. We must remind ourselves that we are His representatives on this earth, and instead of hatred, we must continue to love like God commanded us to love *(John 14:15)*.

Why Hate and Rejection from the World?

Before His departure, Jesus warned His disciples that the world would hate and reject them. No matter how wonderful Jesus's message was, His followers should expect to be rejected because of who they were.

The disciples knew exactly what it meant to be hated by the world. After Jesus departed, they were all persecuted and died as martyrs, except for John. God's enemies tried to kill John by boiling him in oil, but he miraculously survived.

The early Christians knew and had experienced the hatred of the world. We can read their stories in detail in the book *Foxe's Book of Martyrs*. But martyrdom is not a thing of the past. Christians all around the world continue to endure great persecution because of their faith in Christ.

The Friendship of the World (James 4:4)

The world is hostile toward God. And so it follows that it is hostile toward those who believe in God. Jesus tried to comfort His disciples by telling them that the world's hatred was first directed toward Him.

Then Jesus went on to explain further why the world would hate those who believe in Him. He said, "Because you are not of the world." Yes, we are still in this world, but we are not of this world.

God chose us out of this world, and we are, in many ways, different from the world. Therefore, the world hates us.

We Are at War with the World (Ephesians 6:12)

Considering every Christian is a part of a spiritual war, we should not trust any unbeliever to give godly or biblical instructions. They don't have your best interest in mind.

God gave us every remedy for ailments in nature. They are called essential oils. Why trust doctors that believe people are getting better and better when in reality, we are decaying? Doctors, most of the time, are peddling snake oils in the form of petroleum-based pharmaceuticals that only lead to more issues.

Christians Are at War with the World (Ephesians 6:11–15)

Why not use what God has given us in nature? Because they hate God, and they will persecute Christians. The socialists hate God because they want an all-powerful government.

Some religions hate God because they want people to keep trying to earn salvation. Atheists hate God because there is suffering in the world. As we are getting closer and closer to the return of Jesus, persecution of Christians will only increase, including in America.

How should Christians respond? God wants us to love our enemies so they may see God's love for humanity. We are sheep amongst wolves (Matthew 10:16).

Don't try for retribution. God will take care of that. God does want us to be wise to their wicked methods.

Remember, Satan is the God of this World (2 Corinthians 4:4)

They hate God because they are children of Satan. Satan hates people in general because they are made in God's image. That is why Satan wants all people to be dead.

The pharmaceutical industry has been using aborted babies in vaccines for years. When people take those vaccines, doesn't that make them a cannibal or at least an accomplice to murder?

Satan is behind the murder of people, however it happens. Because they hate God, division will occur. Why is the world so divided? Too many people are believing the lies that Dr. Fascinating, Bill Gates, President Biden, the pharmaceutical industry, etc. actually care and want your best interest.

My Closing Words

God created you. God loves you. We sinned, but Jesus died to save you from your sin. If you have never received this free gift of salvation, why not now before it is too late? To every Christian, when persecution comes to you, take heart; God is with you. He will enable you to speak for Him.

We do not need to fear what this world can do to our bodies. We must remember that when we die, we will be with God, as 2 Corinthians 5:8 says. We have nothing to fear when God is with us. How much faith do we have?

Take heart. Jesus has overcome the world (John 16:33). God sent us into this world, and He will enable us to be overcomers. Praise God!

Why Do So Many People Hate God? For What and Why?

> As he journeyed, he came near Damascus, and suddenly, a light shone around him from heaven.
>
> Then he fell to the ground and heard a voice saying to him, "Saul, Saul, why are you persecuting Me?"
>
> And he said, "Who are You, Lord?"
>
> Then the Lord said, "I am Jesus, whom you are persecuting. It is hard for you to kick against the goads."
>
> So he, trembling and astonished, said, "Lord, what do you want me to do?" Then the Lord said to him, "Arise and go into the city, and you will be told what you must do." (Acts 9:3–6)

Those who persecute Christians persecute Christ Himself. This is clearly so since when Jesus appeared to Saul, He did not ask, "Why are you persecuting my people?" Rather, he asked, "Why are you persecuting me?"

It is no stretch to likewise understand that people who hate Christians hate Jesus.

We might wonder why people hatefully persecute Christians. After all, Christians pose no threat to nonbelievers, at least not in obvious ways. Christians are not usually violent. They are usually quiet citizens who mind their own business. So why the hatred?

It is because all unsaved people are enemies of Christ, as the Apostle Paul says in Romans 5:10. How and why?

Even those who ignore God are His enemies because He, being God, must be worshiped. To insist that He does not exist or even to ignore Him is a supreme insult to God by those created by Him to worship Him.

What could be worse? To physically attack Jesus. But since that is impossible, those who hate Him, hate and attack—or persecute—His people. Christians pose no physical threat to the unbelieving world, except that the presence of Christians is an uncomfortable reminder of God, who the world hates.

Last question. Why do some people hate God so much? Because sinful hearts, obsessed with personal autonomy, refuse to acknowledge and bow before Him.

Let us pray for our persecuted brothers and sisters, knowing that while we do not currently incur violent persecution, it could happen here. And let us pray for the persecutors that God would do to many of them what He did to Saul of Tarsus: converting a hater of Christ and a persecutor of His people into a lover of Christ and a servant to His people.

God's Word on Hatred in the Bible

Overcoming hatred is a particular need in today's world. We are divided by race, class, gender, and ideology. The Bible holds the key. And remember, the Bible is right! Let God be true and every man a lie.

Introduction

A. Hate is a sin that has caused many atrocities in our world in the past and in our present time.
B. Hate is a heart ailment forbidden by the Lord in the Old and New Testament.
    1. "Thou shalt not hate thy brother in thine heart" (*Leviticus 19:17*)
    2. *Matthew 5:43–44*

Discussion:

Let's get into the heart of this hatred.

A. *Those that have overcome hatred hate sin, but love the sinner.*
    1. God hates sin.
        a. "These six things doth the LORD hate: yea, seven are an abomination unto him: A proud look, a lying tongue, and hands that shed innocent blood, An heart that deviseth wicked imaginations, feet that be swift in running to mis-

chief, A false witness that speaketh lies, and he that soweth discord among brethren" (*Proverbs 6:16–19*).

    b. *Hebrews 1:9*

2. But God loves the sinner.

    a. *1 John 4:8–11*

    b. *Romans 6:6–8*

3. God wants His children to hate sin.

    a. "Ye that love the LORD, hate evil: he preserveth the souls of his saints; he delivereth them out of the hand of the wicked" (*Psalm 97:10*).

    b. "Hate the evil, and love the good, and establish judgment in the gate: it may be that the LORD God of hosts will be gracious unto the remnant of Joseph" (*Amos 5:15*).

4. Explaining how it was possible to hate what a man did but not the man, let me explain. "It occurred to me that there was one man for whom I had been doing this all my life—myself."

5. We must be careful that we do not transfer our hate for sin to the sinner.

B. *When overcoming hatred, we acknowledge the nature of hate.*

1. Hate is a characteristic of the unregenerate state

    a. *Titus 3:3*

    b. Christians are not to be hateful. Actually, no one

2. Hatred is among the works of the flesh (Galatians 5:19–21).

    a. In this list of sins, hatred is associated with adultery, fornication, murder, drunkenness, and other vices.

    b. Then Paul said (*Galatians 5:21*)

3. Hatred is harbored only by fools. "He that hideth hatred with lying lips, and he that uttereth a slander, is a fool" (*Proverbs 10:18*).

4. *Hatred is cruel.*
   a. "Consider mine enemies; for they are many, and they hate me with cruel hatred" (Psalm 25:19).
   b. In its cruelty, hatred led to the murder of Abel (1 John 3:11–15).
5. Hatred is evidence of immaturity.
   a. *Matthew 5:43–48*
   b. The word *perfect* in this text comes from *teleios* and means *mature.*
   c. Hence, to be mature, we must love—not hate—even our enemies.
   d. Conversely, if we hate rather than love, we indicate our spiritual immaturity.

C. *Failure in overcoming hatred leads to many other evils.*
   1. Hate stirs up trouble.
      a. "Hatred stirreth up strifes: but love covereth all sins" (*Proverbs 10:12*).
      b. The strife that generated between Joseph and his brethren generated from hearts of hate. "And when his brethren saw that their father loved him more than all his brethren, they hated him, and could not speak peaceably unto him. And Joseph dreamed a dream, and he told it his brethren: and they hated him yet the more" (Genesis 37:4–5).
      c. Oftentimes, congregations are torn asunder by strife and turmoil because brethren, instead of loving one another, hate, detest, and despise each other.
   2. Hate generates envy and envy generates hate.
      a. Joseph's brothers hated him (*Genesis 37:8*); and, correspondingly, they envied him (*Genesis 37:11*).

      b. In *Ezekiel 35:11*, God spoke of the envy which Matthew Seir used out of their hatred against Israel.

      c. Indeed, malice, envy, jealousy, ill will, and suspicion all are offspring of hate.

3. Hate leads to murder and assassination.

      a. Because they hated him, Joseph's brothers said, "Let us slay him" (Genesis 37:20).

      b. Too, it is said of him, "The archers have sorely grieved him, and shot at him, and hated him" (Genesis 49:23).

      c. Absalom hated Amnon and had him killed (2 Samuel 13:21–29).

      d. The sins of hatred crucified Jesus (John 15:19–25)

      e. 1 John 3:15

4. Hate leads to sins of the tongue.

      a. David said, "They compassed me about also with words of hatred; and fought against me without a cause" (*Psalm 109:3*).

      b. Solomon said, "He that hateth dissembleth with his lips." "A lying tongue hateth those that are afflicted by it" (*Proverbs 26:24, 28*)

      c. Lying, gossiping, faultfinding, etc. all too often generate from a heart of hate.

      d. Matthew 12:36–37

5. Hate leads to bitterness, resentment and retaliation.

      a. God forbids such

           1) Romans 12:14, 17–21

           2) Matthew 5:38–48

      b. It is important to remember that:

           1) To render evil for evil is devilish

           2) To render good for good is human

           3) But to return good for evil is godlike

D. *Consequences if not overcoming hatred*
   1. Hate will rob you of happiness
      a. As long as you hate, you will be miserable.
      b. Hate and hell dwell in the same heart.
      c. If I were going to knock on the door of the most miserable man in town, I know exactly where I would go—to the door of the bitter, resentful, unforgiving hater.
   2. Hate will make you a slave.
      a. Hate someone, and they will control your thoughts and dreams
      b. Hate someone, and he will require you to take medicine for indigestion, headaches, and loss of energy
      c. If you want to be a slave to someone, find someone to hate.
   3. Hate will harm you physically.
      a. Men sometimes think that it pays to hate, but later, they learn they must pay for hate.
      b. I personally speak of jealousy, envy, self-centeredness, rage, resentment, and hatred as "disease-producing emotions," and he says, "What a person eats is not as important as the bitter spirit, the hates, and feelings of guilt that eat at him."
   4. Hate will keep you out of heaven.
      a. Hate is one of the works of the flesh, and Paul says, "That they which do such things shall not inherit the kingdom of God" (Galatians 5:19–21).
      b. If we hate, we are a murderer, and "no murderer hath eternal life abiding in him" (1 John 3:15).
      c. Finally in this message on hatred…

E. *Love is the way of overcoming hatred.*
   1. With the Bible writers, there is no middle ground between love and hate.
      a. It is either love or hate.
      b. 1 John 2:9–11; 3:14–15
   2. Notice the importance and necessity of love:
      a. Brotherly love is the badge of discipleship (John 13:35).
      b. Brotherly love is a command (John 15:12).
      c. Brotherly love is to be maintained above all things (1 Peter 4:8).
      d. Brotherly love is the second greatest commandment (Matthew 22:39).
      e. Brotherly love is a fulfilling of the law (Romans 13:8).
      f. Brotherly love will prevent stumbling (1 John 2:9–11).
      g. Brotherly love is a mark of divine sonship (1 John 3:10).
   3. What is the nature of the love we are to have for our brethren?
      a. We are love the brethren as the Lord loved us (John 13:34).
      b. We are to love the brethren as ourselves (Matthew 22:39).
      c. We are to love the brethren fervently (1 Peter 4:8).
      d. We are to love the brethren without hypocrisy (1 Peter 1:22–23).
      e. We are to love the brethren in deed and not word only (1 John 3:18).

Conclusion (End of this sermon on hatred):

A. If we hate someone, to overcome this we should:
   1. Pray for the person who is the object of our hate

2. Find something good to do for the person who is resented
3. Try sincerely to understand the person who is disliked and resented

B. Solomon said, "Better is a dinner of herbs where love is, than a stalled ox and hatred therewith" (Proverbs 15:17).

C. With Booker T. Washington, let us say, "I will not allow any man to reduce my soul to the level of hatred."

God Created This World

If God had created a world without violence, it also would have been a world without freedom. God, in His love, gave us the freedom to choose. Our freedoms have brought about a lot of the suffering apparent in the world.

God is personally involved in the affairs of the world. He entered this world as a human person and allowed himself to experience pain and suffering right along with us. His plan is to heal the world one day, for good, to take away all hatred and violence. Ultimately, we don't know why there is hatred and violence, but isn't it better to go through life with God than without Him?

Jesus would give an answer like the story of the Good Samaritan. "Love your neighbor as yourself." The man answers, "Who is my neighbor?"

The problem is that we are selfish, and we only think about ourselves. We try to define what we think is good, and we choose what is best for us, not our neighbors. We don't love our neighbors well.

God is not a monster; God is love. God is aware, and He cares. God takes all of the pain on Himself and feels it all very deeply. He offers solutions to the brokenness instead of turning His back on it.

When using the four worlds, the part that really speaks to this question is when talking about relationships. God created us out of love to be in harmony with Himself, with each other, and with the world around us. But we have been separated from God, destroyed relationships with each other and don't live in harmony with the world because of our selfishness and brokenness.

The World's Hatred on God

The world hates God, so they are a threat to Christians!

This is very clear, not only from the *Scriptures*, but based on everything that's going on around us. But this should not come as a surprise to all *followers* of Jesus Christ.

In *John 15:18–19*, remember how it all started: "If the world hates you, you know that it hated Me before it hated you. If you were of the world, the world would love its own. Yet because you are not of the world, but I chose you out of the world, therefore the world hates you."

Jesus Teaches His Disciples Hate and Rejection from the World

Before His departure, Jesus warned His disciples that *the world would hate and reject them*. No matter how wonderful Jesus's message was, His followers should expect to be rejected because of who they are.

The disciples knew exactly what it meant *to be hated* by the *world*. After Jesus departed, they were *all persecuted* and *died* as *martyrs*, except for John. God's *enemies* tried *to kill John*.

The early Christians knew and had experienced *the hatred of the world*. We can read their stories in detail in the Bible. Of the martyrs: martyrdom is not a thing of the past. Christians all around the world continue to endure great persecution because of their faith in Christ.

In this World But Not of This World

The world is hostile toward God. And so it follows that it is hostile toward those who believe in God. Jesus tried to comfort His disciples by telling them that *the world's hatred was first directed toward Him.*

Then Jesus went on to explain further why the world would *hate* those who believe in Him. He said, "Because you are not of the world." Yes, we are still in this *world*, but we are not of this world.

God chose us out of this world, and we are, in many ways, different from the world. Therefore, *the world hates us.*

At War with the World

Considering every Christian is a part of a spiritual war, we should not trust any unbeliever to give godly or biblical instructions. They don't have your best interest in mind.

God gave us every remedy for ailments in nature. They are called essential oils and prayers. Thank God for doctors that believe people are getting better and better because of God's knowledge. Doctors, most of the time, are gifts from God. He created them to study the human body. It's God's love.

Christians Are at War with the World

Why not use what God has given us in nature? *Because they hate God,* and they will persecute Christians. *The socialists hate God* because they want an all-powerful government.

The world hates God because the Christians they want people to keep trying to earn salvation. *Atheists hate God* because there is suffering in the world. As we are getting closer and closer to the return of Jesus, persecution of Christians will only increase, including in America.

How should Christians respond? God wants us *to love our enemies so they may see God's love for humanity. We are sheep amongst wolves* (Matthew 10:16).

Don't try for retribution. God will take care of that. God doesn't want us to be wise to their wicked methods.

Satan is the God of this World (2 Corinthians 4:4): A Reminder

They hate God because they are children of Satan. Satan hates people in general because they were made *in God's image*. That is why Satan wants all people to be dead (John 8:44, John 10:10).

The pharmaceutical industry has been using aborted babies in vaccines for years. When people take those vaccines, doesn't that make them a cannibal or at least an accomplice to murder?

Satan is behind the murder of people, however it happens. Because *they hate God*, division will occur. Why is the world so divided? Too many people are believing the lies of Satan. He comes to steal, kill, and destroy (John 10:10).

My Final Words

People lie just to stay in power, but they don't believe in God's power! Christians are commanded not to love the world but love the people in the world. What we should not love are the sins of the people of the world (*1 John 2:15*).

My Final Words

God created you. God loves you. We sinned, but Jesus died to save you from your sin. If you have never received this free gift of salvation, why not now before it is too late? To every Christian, when persecution comes to you, take heart. God is with you. He will enable you to speak for Him (*Matthew 5:10–12*)

We do not need to fear what this world can do to our bodies. We must remember that when we die, we will be with God as *2 Corinthians 5:7–8* says. We have nothing to fear when God is with us. How much faith do we have? God will take great care of us. (*1 Peter 5:7*).

Much love, much prayers always.

About the Author

Pastor Freddie E. Dixson Sr. was born in New Orleans, Louisiana, on October 2, 1952, to Walter and Angelette Dixson. He had six siblings. He attended school in Orleans Parish, served in the US Air Force, with an honorable discharge. Two years later, in the year 1993, he enrolled in Christian Bible College and studied for four years on counseling, Old Testament, and The New Testament survey of the books of the Bible. He also studied the doctrine of Jesus Christ. He graduated in the year 1997 with a Ba. Thd. He coached biddies, north playground boys, and girls' basketball. He worked at Coca-Cola in Harahan, Louisiana, for thirty-six years.

He now pastors the Mt. Zion Baptist Church in Saint Rose, Louisiana. He enjoys witnessing for the Lord. He has been blessed to be married to the love of his life, Sis. Marlene M. Dixson, for forty-two years. God has blessed them with two sons, Dedric E. Dixson Sr. and Freddie E. Dixson Jr. They are blessed with four beautiful grandkids, who he teach the Word of God. He is also a counselor for couples who anticipate marriage.

On his spare time, he is playing basketball with his grandkids. He loves reading the Bible. He hosts a prayer line request on Mondays. He loves teaching God's Word to the congregation as well as the community of Saint Rose, Louisiana, and definitely loves giving back to the community. He and his wife enjoy helping the unfortunate, those who are destitute. They enjoy feeding the homeless and the birds etc. But most importantly, they thank God for the gift of His Son, Jesus Christ, for giving him and his family and relatives life and a more abundant life. He hopes that God will continue to use him in writing more books and that it will help the people of this world to accept Jesus Christ as their personal Savior. "Thanks for all you do. The Lord's rewards are for you. God bless!"